EASY TRADITIONAL QUILTS

Log Cabins

by Christiane Meunier

CHITRA PUBLICATIONS

Your Best Value in Quilting!

Copyright © 1999 by Christiane Meunier

All Rights Reserved. Published in the United States of America.

Printed in Hong Kong.

Chitra Publications

2 Public Avenue

Montrose, Pennsylvania 18801-1220

First printing: 1999

Library of Congress Cataloging-in-Publication Data

Meunier, Christiane, 1952-

Easy traditional quilts.   Log Cabins/Christiane Meunier.

p. cm.

ISBN 1-885588-26-7

1. Patchwork--Patterns. 2. Patchwork quilts.   1.   Title

TT835.M487   1998

746.46'041--dc21   98-28543

CIP

Edited by: Elsie Campbell

Design & Illustrations: Kimberly L. Grace

Cover and Inside Photography: Van Zandbergen Photography, Brackney, PA

Our Mission Statement

We publish quality quilting magazines and books that recognize, promote and inspire self-expression. We are dedicated to serving our customers with respect, kindness and efficiency.

Welcome to
Easy Traditional Quilts: Log Cabins

I find this all-time favorite quilt pattern endlessly fascinating. Not only is it easy to piece, but it also takes on many different looks from simple variations in the block setting. Whether you prefer Barn Raising, Straight Furrows or Light and Dark, all are dynamic sets with lots of visual appeal.

Depending on your fabric choices, a Log Cabin quilt can have a feel that ranges from antique to contemporary or country-style to formal. It's a most accommodating pattern! It's fun to achieve contrasts with fabrics to give Log Cabin blocks their "personality."

At first glance, the block may seem simple and unassuming. It has surprising subtleties and variations, however. For instance, simply varying the strip width from one side of the block to the other can create the illusion of curves. Susanne McCoy's "Full Circle II: Contrast" on page 15 illustrates this. The Pineapple block is an exciting variation of the Log Cabin design and you'll find a pattern for one that's foundation pieced on page 29.

While making several of the quilts in this pattern book, I found the lure of experimenting with the block irresistible. Ideas popped into my head at a rapid rate when I asked myself "What if…?" That's the provocative question that precedes all of our "Design Challenges" in *Traditional Quiltworks* magazine. Answering it led me to some unique twists for this classic block such as piecing the logs in "Sunny Windows" (page 10) to create a new look. Or try my "Crazy Maze Log Cabin" on page 21 if you feel like stepping out of the confines of a traditional-looking log cabin block.

These 11 patterns offer a variety of construction techniques, including rotary cutting, foundation piecing and templates. So turn the pages for some inspiring quilts and patterns that practically guarantee stitching success. I'm sure that your Log Cabin quilts made using these patterns will win rave reviews.

Christiane

Table of Contents

Pattern Ratings

Beginner   Intermediate   Advanced

Blue Star Log Cabin

Warm any room with logs made of rich dark colors combined with lighter tones.

QUILT SIZE: 87 1/2" x 98 3/4"
BLOCK SIZE: 11 1/4" square

MATERIALS

Yardage is estimated for 44" fabric.
- 2/3 yard medium gold print, for the center squares and the middle border NOTE: *This is enough fabric for pieced border strips. If you wish to cut your borders in continuous strips, you will need 2 1/2 yards. Cut the lengthwise border strips before cutting the center squares.*
- 1/2 yard each of 2 light green prints, 1 light red print, 2 dark red prints, 2 light gold prints, 4 brown prints, 2 dark blue prints and 1 light blue print
- 5/8 yard each of 2 dark green prints, 2 navy prints and 1 gray-blue print
- 3 1/4 yards navy print for the borders and binding
- 7 3/4 yards backing fabric
- 92" x 103" piece of batting

CUTTING

All dimensions include a 1/4" seam allowance.
- Cut 42: 2 3/4" squares, gold print, for the centers of the blocks
- Cut 8: 1 1/2" x 44" strips, gold print, for the middle border
- Cut 7: 1 1/4" x 44" strips, from each light green print
- Cut 14: 1 1/4" x 44" strips, from each dark green print
- Cut 12: 1 1/4" x 44" strips, from the light red print
- Cut 12: 1 1/4" x 44" strips, from each dark red print
- Cut 4: 1 1/4" x 44" strips, from each light gold print
- Cut 4: 1 1/4" x 44" strips, from each brown print
- Cut 12: 1 1/4" x 44" strips, light blue print
- Cut 12: 1 1/4" x 44" strips, from each dark blue print
- Cut 16: 1 1/4" x 44" strips, gray-blue

print
- Cut 16: 1 1/4" x 44" strips, from each navy print
- Cut 2: 2 1/2" x 74" lengthwise strips, navy print, for the inner border
- Cut 2: 2 1/2" x 80" lengthwise strips, navy print, for the inner border
- Cut 2: 6 3/4" x 90" lengthwise strips, navy print, for the outer border
- Cut 2: 6 3/4" x 88" lengthwise strips, navy print, for the outer border
- Cut 5: 2 1/2" x 80" lengthwise strips, navy print, for the binding

PREPARATION

To make the pieced panels:
- Stitch a 1 1/4" x 44" light green print strip between two 1 1/4" x 44"  dark green print strips to make a pieced panel. Press the seam allowances toward the dark fabric. Make 14.
- In the same manner, make 12 red print panels, 8 light gold print and brown print panels, 12 light blue print and dark blue print panels and 16 gray-blue print and navy print panels. Refer to the photo for color placement, as needed.

PIECING

For 4 red/green blocks:
- Place a 2 3/4" gold print square, right sides together, on a red print panel aligning the right edges. Stitch them together and stop with the needle down. Chain sew 3 more 2 3/4" gold print squares to the panel, as shown.

- Cut the red panel between the squares and after the last square sewn, yielding 4 pieced units. Press the 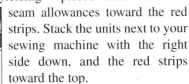 seam allowances toward the red strips. Stack the units next to your sewing machine with the right side down, and the red strips toward the top.

- Chain sew the units to a red panel, as shown.
- Cut them apart, as before. Press the seam allowances toward the last strip added. Stack them right side down, with the last strip added toward the top.
- Chain sew them to a green panel. Cut them apart. Press, as before. Stack them with the last strip added toward the top.
- Chain sew the units to the green panel once more so there are 2 red panel strips on each of 2 adjacent sides and 2 green panel strips on each of the opposite sides of the blocks, as shown.

For 10 brown/green blocks:
- Sew a 2 3/4" gold print square to a brown panel as for the red/green blocks. Chain sew 9 more gold print squares to the panel.
- Cut the brown panel between the squares and after the last square sewn, to yield 10 pieced units. Press the seam allowances toward the brown strips. Stack them right side down, with the brown strips toward the top.
- In the same manner as for the red/green blocks, continue sewing additional brown panel strips and green panel strips to the blocks until there are 2 panel strips of each color on each side, as shown.

I selected prints that read as solids from a distance for the pieced panels used to make this handsome log cabin quilt. Set in the Barn Raising pattern, **"Blue Star Log Cabin"** *(87 1/2" x 98 3/4") will really bring you "blue ribbon" accolades!*

For 12 red/light blue blocks:

• Sew a 2 3/4" gold print square to a red panel, as before. Sew 11 more gold print squares to the panel.

Cut, press, and stack the units, as before. Continue in this manner, sewing additional red panel strips, and light blue panel strips, as shown.

For 16 brown/navy blocks:

Sew a 2 3/4" gold print square to a brown panel, as before. Sew 15 more gold print squares to the panel.

Cut, press, and stack the units, as before. Continue in this manner, sewing additional brown panel strips and navy panel strips, as shown.

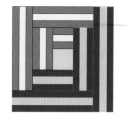

ASSEMBLY

• Referring to the photo, lay out the blocks in 7 rows of 6.

• Sew the blocks into rows and join the rows.

• Measure the length of the quilt. Trim the 2 1/2" x 80" navy print strips to that measurement. Sew them to the long sides of the quilt.

• Measure the width of the quilt including the borders. Trim the 2 1/2" x 74" navy print strips to that measurement. Sew them to the remaining sides of the quilt.

• Sew two 1 1/2" x 44" gold print strips together end to end, to make a pieced border. Make 4.

• Measure the length of the quilt. Trim

two gold pieced borders to that measurement. Sew them to the long sides of the quilt.

• In the same manner, trim the remaining gold pieced borders to fit the quilt's width and sew them to the remaining sides of the quilt.

• Trim the 6 3/4" x 90" navy print strips to fit the quilt's length and sew them to the long sides of the quilt.

• Trim the 6 3/4" x 88" navy print strips to fit the quilt's width and sew them to the remaining sides of the quilt.

• Finish the quilt as described in *General Directions*, using the 2 1/2" x 80" navy print strips for the binding.

Peppermint & Sassafras

A pink and brown twist to an old favorite!

QUILT SIZE: 72" x 90"
BLOCK SIZE: 9" square

MATERIALS

Yardage is estimated for 44" fabric.
- 1/2 yard very light brown print
- 3/4 yard light brown print
- 1 1/4 yards medium brown print
- 1 3/4 yards dark brown print
- 3/4 yard very light pink print
- 1 1/8 yards light pink print
- 1 1/2 yards medium pink print
- 2 yards dark pink print
- 1 yard dark brown solid, for the center squares and binding
- 5 1/2 yards backing fabric
- 76" x 94" piece of batting

CUTTING

- Cut 9: 1 1/2" x 44" strips, very light brown print
- Cut 16: 1 1/2" x 44" strips, light brown print
- Cut 23: 1 1/2" x 44" strips, medium brown print
- Cut 32: 1 1/2" x 44" strips, dark brown print
- Cut 12: 1 1/2" x 44" strips, very light pink print
- Cut 20: 1 1/2" x 44" strips, light pink print
- Cut 29: 1 1/2" x 44" strips, medium pink print
- Cut 36: 1 1/2" x 44" strips, dark pink print
- Cut 80: 1 1/2" squares, dark brown solid
- Cut 8: 2 1/2" x 44" strips, dark brown solid, for the binding

DIRECTIONS

To quickly construct this block, I suggest chain piecing the same step on all 80 blocks before moving on to the next step. After each step, cut between the units, open, press, and stack them right side down, so that all units are in identical position. This little saying will come in handy as you stack the blocks: "The last piece added is always on the bottom". It will also be perpendicular to the next strip that you will add. When stitching, be sure to leave only a small space (about 1/16") between units. When there is not enough strip left to fit an additional unit, cut this part of the strip off and start another strip. After adding each strip, press the seam away from the center square.

PIECING

- Stitch a 1 1/2" dark brown solid square to a very light brown strip, right sides together. Continue by adding one square after another until all 80 squares are sewn to a very light brown strip.
- Cut between the units, open, press the seam allowance toward the light brown, and stack them right side down, making sure "the last piece added is always on the bottom," as shown. This completes Step 1.

- Stitch the units to the very light brown print strips, right sides together, as shown until all 80 units are stitched.

- Cut between the units, open, press the seam allowance toward the last strip added, and stack the units right side down, making sure "the last piece added is always on the bottom."
- Stitch the units to the very light pink print strips, right sides together, until all 80 units are stitched, as shown.

- Cut between the units, open, press, and stack as before.
- Stitch the units to the very light pink print strips, right sides together, until all 80 units are stitched, as shown.

- Cut between the units, open, press, and stack.

- Continue in the same manner, adding the remaining strips as shown in the block diagram:

5 - light brown print
6 - light brown print
7 - light pink print
8 - light pink print
9 - medium brown print
10 - medium brown print
11 - medium pink print
12 - medium pink print
13 - dark brown print
14 - dark brown print
15 - dark pink print
16 - dark pink print

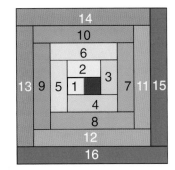

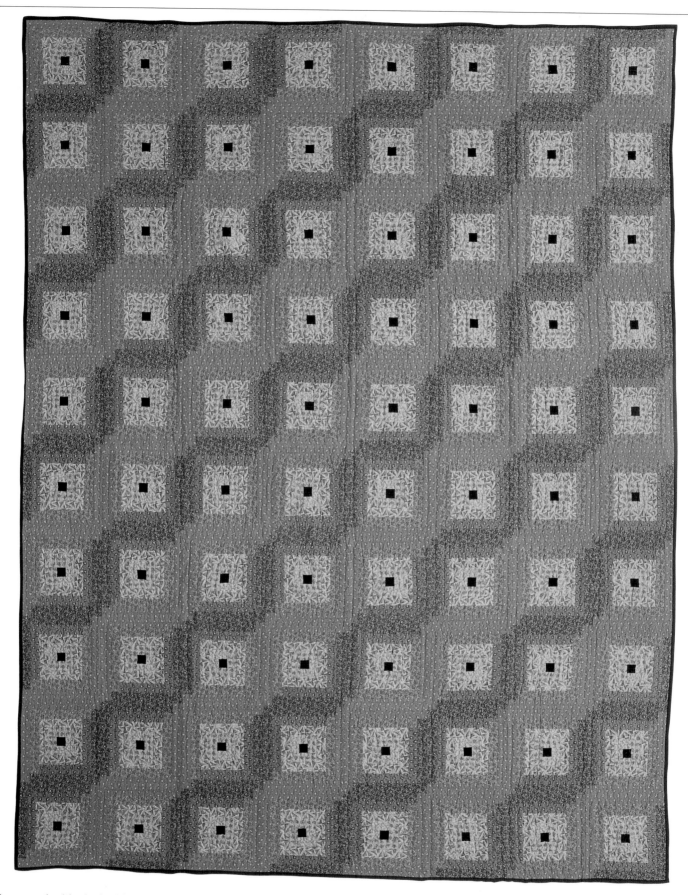

Lay out the blocks in 10 rows of 8, referring to the photo.
Stitch the blocks into rows. Join the rows.
Finish the quilt as described in *General Directions,*
~~s~~ing the 2 1/2" x 44" solid dark brown strips for the binding.

Roxanne Rentzel of Van Alstyne, Texas, immediately envisioned a Log Cabin quilt when she found these pink and brown fabrics in a shop. **"Peppermint and Sassafras"** *(72" x 90"), named after the Marcus Brothers fabric collection with the same name, reminds Roxanne of a quilt that would have been seen in the old west.*

Shirley's Log Cabin

Create a unique design from a common block!

QUILT SIZE: 73 1/2" x 96"
BLOCK SIZE: 11 1/4" square

MATERIALS

Yardage is estimated for 44" fabric. Assign the fabrics a number, as indicated, for easier identification in cutting the strips and sewing the blocks. It may be helpful to attach a small swatch of each fabric to an index card and label it for easy reference.

- 1/8 yard red
- 1 yard light blue plaid #1
- 1/2 yard light blue plaid #2
- 1/2 yard light blue plaid #3
- 1 1/4 yards light blue plaid #4
- 1/3 yard light blue plaid #5
- 1/2 yard medium blue plaid #6
- 1 yard medium blue plaid #7
- 3/4 yard medium blue plaid #8
- 1 yard small red check #9, for the blocks and binding
- 3/4 yard large red plaid #10
- 2 1/4 yards dark blue check #11 for the blocks, border and binding
- 5 2/3 yards backing fabric
- 78" x 100" piece of batting

CUTTING

Dimensions include a 1/4" seam allowance.
For the blocks:
- Cut 48: 1 3/4" squares, red
- Cut 15: 1 3/4" x 44" strips, light blue plaid #1
- Cut 9: 1 3/4" x 44" strips, light blue plaid #2
- Cut 9: 1 3/4" x 44" strips, light blue plaid #3
- Cut 21: 1 3/4" x 44" strips, light blue plaid #4
- Cut 6: 1 3/4" x 44" strips, light blue plaid #5
- Cut 9: 1 3/4" x 44" strips, medium blue plaid #6
- Cut 15: 1 3/4" x 44" strips, medium blue plaid #7
- Cut 11: 1 3/4" x 44" strips, medium blue plaid #8

- Cut 14: 1 3/4" x 44" strips, small red check #9
- Cut 11: 1 3/4" x 44" strips, large red plaid #10
- Cut 16: 1 3/4" x 44" strips, dark blue check #11
Also:
- Cut 8: 3" x 44" strips, dark blue check, for the border
- Cut 6: 2 1/2" x 44" strips, dark blue check, for the binding
- Cut 3: 2 1/2" x 44" strips, small red check, for the binding
NOTE: *Shirley made a two-color binding for her quilt. If you prefer to use one color, cut a total of nine 2 1/2" x 44" strips from the dark blue check.*

PIECING
For 24 A Blocks:
- Sew a 1 3/4" red square to a #1 strip, right sides together. Without cutting them apart, sew the rest of the red squares to the strip, one at a time, leaving 1/16" between them.

- Cut the strip between the red squares to yield 24 pieced units.

- Press all seam allowances away from the red center, toward the outside of the block.

- Stack the units, all in the same direction. Lay the stack beside you, right side down, with the blue plaid toward you.
- Chain sew these units to a #1 strip, as before. Start another #1 strip when the first one runs out.

- Cut the strips between each unit. Press and stack the units and lay the stack beside you, right side down, with the last strip added toward you.
- Chain sew these units to a #6 strip, as before. Cut them apart and stack them beside you, right side down, with the last strip added toward you.

- Continue adding strips to the units in a clockwise direction, referring to the Block A diagram on page 10.

(Continued on page 10)

*In response to a special request from her daughter, Shirley Malia of Owego, New York, stitched **"Log Cabin"** (73 1/2" x 96").
This quilt was made to resemble an antique. Though the blocks are laid out in a traditional Barn Raising setting, a secondary
pattern emerges. A dark strip on the outside of half the blocks creates this design.*

9

(Continued from page 8)

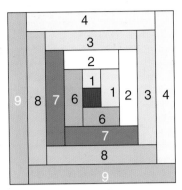

Block A

For 24 B Blocks:
• Make Block B in the same manner, using the remaining red squares for the centers. Refer to the Block B diagram for fabric placement.

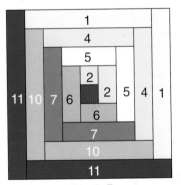

Block B

• Referring to the photo, lay out the blocks in 8 rows of 6.
• Sew the blocks into rows and join the rows.
• Sew two 3" x 44" dark blue check strips together, end to end, to make a border. Make 4.
• Measure the length of the quilt. Trim 2 borders to that measurement. Set aside the scrap pieces. Sew the borders to the long sides of the quilt.
• Stitch a border scrap piece, end to end, to each remaining border.
• Measure the width of the quilt. Trim the borders to that measurement. Sew them to the remaining sides of the quilt.
• Finish the quilt as described in *General Directions*, using the 2 1/2" x 44" dark blue check and small red check strips for the binding. Refer to the quilt photo for placement, as desired.

Sunny Windows
Make your own Sunny Windows in sparkling bright sunshine colors.

QUILT SIZE: 72" x 85 1/2"
BLOCK SIZE: 12 1/2"

MATERIALS
Yardage is estimated for 44" fabric.
• Fat quarter (18" x 22") each of 8 yellow prints, 4 tan prints, 10 green prints and 2 red prints, for the blocks
• 1/8 yard each of 6 blue prints, for the sashing
• 1/4 yard red print, for the block centers and cornerstones
• 1 yard black print, for the blocks and the inner border
• 1/3 yard dark yellow print, for the middle border
• 2 1/8 yards blue print, for the outer border and binding
• 5 yards backing fabric
• 76" x 90" piece of batting

CUTTING
Dimensions include a 1/4" seam allowance. Cut the lengthwise blue print strips before cutting other pieces from that fabric.
For the Log Cabin blocks:
• Cut 1: 1 1/4" x 22" strip, each of 7 green prints. Label them A.
• Cut 1: 2 1/2" x 22" strip, each of 7 green or red prints. Label them C.
• Cut 1: 3 3/4" x 22" strip, each of 7 green or red prints. Label them E.
• Cut 1: 5" x 22" strip, each of 7 green or red prints. Label them G.
• Cut 1: 2 1/2" x 22" strip, each of 7 yellow or tan prints. Label them B.
• Cut 1: 3 3/4" x 22" strip, each of 7 yellow or tan prints. Label them D.
• Cut 1: 5" x 22" strip, each of 7 yellow or tan prints. Label them F.
• Cut 1: 6 1/4" x 22" strip, each of 7 yellow or tan prints. Label them H.
• Cut 14: 1 1/2" x 44" strips, black print, then cut them in quarters across the width to yield fifty-six 1 1/2" x 11" strips

• Cut 20: 3" squares, red print, for the block centers
For the sashing and cornerstones:
• Cut 6: 1 1/2" x 13" strips each of 6 blue prints. You will use 31.
• Cut 12: 1 1/2" squares, red print for the cornerstones
Also:
• Cut 8: 2 1/2" x 44" strips, black print for the inner border
• Cut 8: 1" x 44" strips, dark yellow print, for the middle border
• Cut 4: 7" x 72" lengthwise strips, blue print for the outer border
• Cut 5: 2 1/2" x 72" lengthwise strips, blue print for the binding

DIRECTIONS
• Cut a 1 1/4" x 22" green print strip in half to yield two 1 1/4" x 11" strips. Sew a 1 1/2" x 11" black print strip between them to make a pieced panel. Press the seam allowances toward the black print strip. Make 7.
• Cut six 1 3/4" slices from each pieced panel to yield 42 slices. You will use 40.

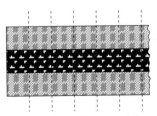

• Group the slices in matching pairs. Label them A. Set them aside.
• In the same manner, cut a 2 1/2" x 22" yellow or tan print strip in half to yield two 2 1/2" x 11" strips. Sew a 1 1/2" x 11" black print strip between them to make a pieced panel. Press the seam allowances toward the black print strip. Make 7.
• Cut six 1 3/4" slices from each pieced panel, as before. Group them in matching pairs. Label them B. Set them aside.
• In the same manner, make pieced panels with the remaining 22"-long green

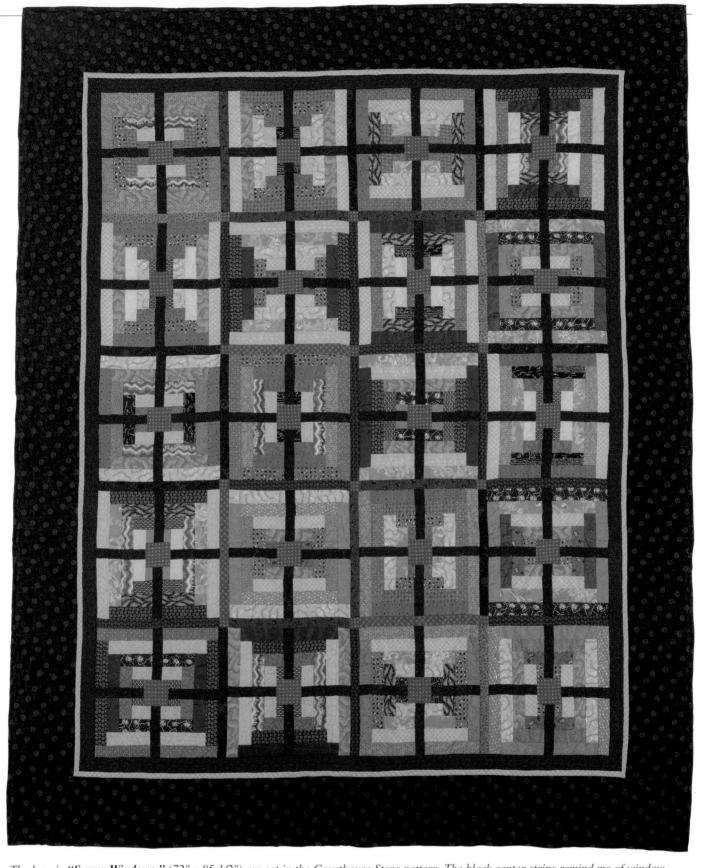

The logs in **"Sunny Windows"** *(72" x 85 1/2") are set in the Courthouse Steps pattern. The black center strips remind me of window pane sashing and the bright, warm colors make this a cheerful and sunny quilt.*

ed, yellow and tan strips, cutting each of them in half and sewing 1 1/2" x 11" black strip between the halves. Cut the pieced pan- ls into 1 3/4" slices, group them in matching pairs and label them s listed in the cutting directions. NOTE: *Press the seam llowances in the E and F panels as before. Press the seam*

allowances in the C, D, G and H panels away from the black print.

For each Log Cabin block:

• Place an A slice on a 3" red print square, right sides together with right edges aligned. Sew them to make a pieced unit.

(Continued from page 11)

Press the seam allowance toward the A.

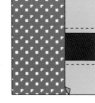

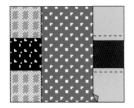

- Lay a matching A slice on the opposite side of the pieced unit, right sides together and sew them, as before. Press the seam allowance toward the A.

- Sew a B slice to each of the long sides of the pieced unit. Press the seam allowances toward the B. This completes round 1.

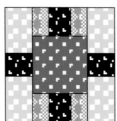

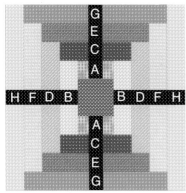

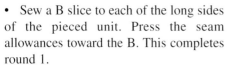

- Sew a green or red print C to each A side of the pieced unit. Press seam allowance toward the C. Continue adding matching pairs of strips to opposite sides of the pieced unit in alphabetical order as shown in the block diagram, to complete a block. Make 20.

ASSEMBLY

- Referring to the photograph, lay out the Log Cabin blocks, 1 1/2" x 13" blue print sashing strips and 1 1/2" red print cornerstones.
- Sew the sashing squares and horizontal sashing strips into rows. Sew the blocks and vertical sashing strips into rows. Join the rows.
- Sew two 2 1/2" x 44" black print strips together, end to end, to make an inner border. Make 4.
- Measure the length of the quilt. Trim 2 inner borders to that measurement. Sew them to the long sides of the quilt.
- Measure the width of the quilt, including the borders. Trim the remaining inner borders to that measurement. Sew them to the remaining sides of the quilt.
- Sew two 1" x 44" dark yellow print strips together, end to end, to make a middle border. Make 4.
- Measure the length of the quilt. Trim 2 middle borders to that measurement. Sew them to the long sides of the quilt.
- Measure the width of the quilt, including the borders. Trim the remaining middle borders to that measurement. Sew them to the remaining sides of the quilt.
- In the same manner, trim two 7" x 72" blue print strips to fit the quilt's length and sew them to the long sides of the quilt.
- Trim the remaining 7" x 72" blue print strips to fit the quilt's width and sew them to the remaining sides of the quilt.
- Finish the quilt as described in *General Directions*, using the 2 1/2" x 72" blue print strips for the binding.

Cabin in the Stars

The Log Cabin becomes a star!

QUILT SIZE: 47 1/2" x 58"
BLOCK SIZE: 9 1/2" square

MATERIALS

Yardage is estimated for 44" fabric.
- Scraps of light or tan prints totaling approximately 3/4 yard
- Scraps of medium and dark prints and plaids totaling approximately 1 1/4 yards
- 1/8 yard red print
- 1 1/4 yards tan print, for the background
- 1 3/8 yards red check, for the sashing, border and binding
- Glue stick (optional)
- 3 1/2 yards backing fabric
- 52" x 62" piece of batting
- Paper, muslin or lightweight nonfusible interfacing for the foundations

CUTTING

Dimensions include a 1/4" seam allowance. Fabric for foundation piecing will be cut as you sew the blocks. Each piece must be at least 1/4" larger on all sides than the section it will cover. Refer to General Directions *as needed.*
- Cut 2: 1 1/2" x 44" strips, red print, from them cut thirty-two 1 1/2" squares
- Cut 1 3/4" wide strips from the light, medium and dark print scraps

For each of 20 blocks:
- Cut 4: 3 1/4" squares, medium or dark plaid

Also:
- Cut 6: 2 7/8" x 44" strips, tan print, from them cut eighty 2 7/8" squares
- Cut 7: 3 1/4" x 44" strips, tan print, from them cut eighty 3 1/4" squares
- Cut 31: 1 1/2" x 10" strips, red check, for the sashing
- Cut 5: 3 1/2" x 44" strips, red check, for the border
- Cut 6: 2 1/2" x 44" strips, red check, for the binding

DIRECTIONS

For the Log Cabin Squares:
Follow the foundation piecing instructions in General Directions to piece the blocks.

(Continued on page 14)

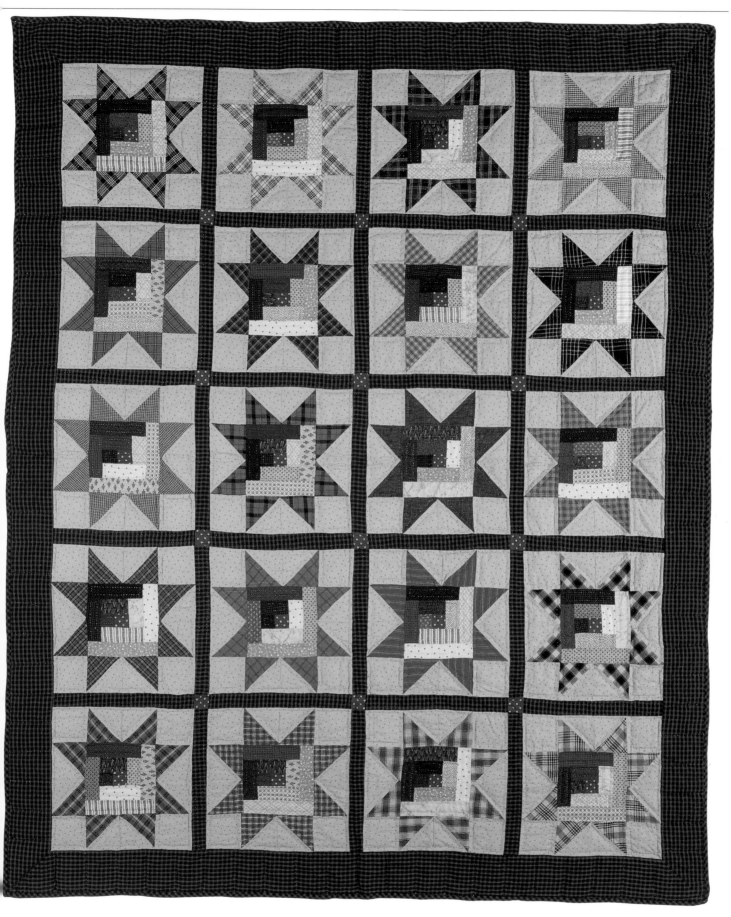

...og Cabin blocks fit neatly inside the enlarged centers of these Sawtooth Stars. Ginny St. Denis of St. Cloud, Florida, gave **"Cabin in the Stars"** *...7 1/2" x 58") a country feel by using several homespun fabrics.*

(Continued from page 12)

• Trace the full size pattern 20 times on the foundation material, transferring all lines and numbers and leaving a 1" space between foundations. Cut each one out 1/2" beyond the broken line.

• Use the following fabrics in these positions:

1 - 1 1/2" red print square
2, 3 - dark
4, 5 - light
6, 7 - dark
8, 9 - light

• Baste each foundation in the seam allowance, halfway between the stitching line and the broken line, to hold the fabrics in place, if desired.

• Trim each foundation on the broken line. Set them aside.

For each Star Log Cabin block:

• Draw a diagonal line, from corner to corner, on the wrong side of each of four 3 1/4" tan print squares.

• Lay a marked square on a 3 1/4" plaid square, right sides together. Sew 1/4" away from the marked line on both sides. Make 4, using the same plaid fabric for all of them.

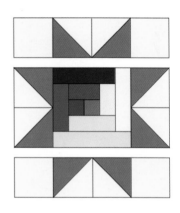

• Cut the squares apart on the marked lin to yield 8 pieced squares. Press the sea allowance toward the plaid.

• Join 2 pieced squares, as shown, t make a star point unit. Make 4.

• Lay out the 4 star point units, four 7/8" tan print squares and a Log Cabi square, as shown. Join them to complete Log Cabin Star block. Make 20.

Full-Size Foundation for Cabin in the Stars.

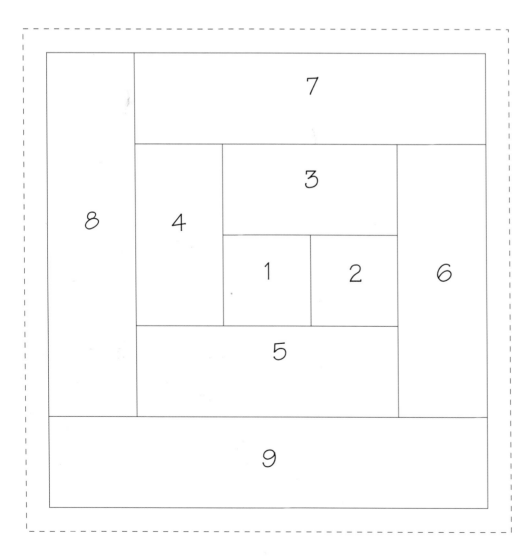

ASSEMBLY

• Referring to the photo, lay out th blocks, 1 1/2" x 10" dark check sashir strips and 1 1/2" red print squares.

• Sew the red print squares and horizont sashing strips into rows. Sew the bloc and vertical sashing strips into rows. Jo the rows.

• Stitch three 3 1/2" x 44" red check stri together, end to end, to make a long bo der strip. Cut the strip in half to yield borders.

• Measure the length of the quilt. Tri borders to that measurement. Set asi the scrap pieces. Sew the borders to t long sides of the quilt.

• Stitch a border scrap piece to each the remaining 3 1/2" x 44" red che strips end to end.

• Measure the width of the quilt. Trim t borders to that measurement. Sew the to the remaining sides of the quilt.

• Finish the quilt as described in *Gener Directions*, using the 2 1/2" x 44" r check strips for the binding.

Full Circle II: Contrast

Create the impression of gentle curves with this off-center block.

"Full Circle II: Contrast" (54 1/2" square) by Susanne McCoy of Washington, D.C. uses only two colors to produce a striking image, with yellow sections that seem to float on a sea of dark blue. The center medallion is taken from the quilt "Borealis" that appeared in Mary Ellen Hopkin's Log Cabin Notebook.

Full Circle II: Contrast

QUILT SIZE: 54 1/2" square
BLOCK SIZE: 6 3/4" square

MATERIALS

Yardage is estimated for 44" fabric.
- 1 1/2 yards assorted yellow prints
- 2 1/2 yards assorted blue prints
- 1/2 yard blue print for the binding
- 3 1/2 yards backing fabric
- 59" square of batting
- Paper, muslin or lightweight nonfusible interfacing for the foundations

CUTTING

Dimensions include a 1/4" seam allowance. Fabric for foundation piecing will be cut as you sew the blocks. Each piece must be at least 1/4" larger on all sides than the section it will cover. Refer to General Directions *as needed.*
- Cut 16: 2" squares, assorted yellow prints
- Cut 48: 2" squares, assorted blue prints
- Cut 6: 2 1/2" x 44" strips, blue print for the binding

DIRECTIONS

Follow the foundation piecing instructions in General Directions *to piece the blocks.*
- Trace the full-size pattern (on page 17) 64 times on the foundation material, transferring all lines and numbers and leaving a 1" space between foundations. Cut each one out 1/2" beyond the broken line.

For each of 28 A Blocks:
- Use the following fabrics in these positions:
  - 1 - 2" blue print square
  - 2, 3 - yellow prints
  - 4, 5 - blue prints
  - 6, 7 - yellow prints
  - 8, 9 - blue prints
  - 10, 11 - yellow prints

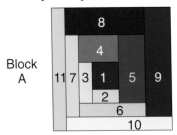

Block A

For each of 12 B Blocks:
- Use the following fabrics in these positions:
  - 1 - 2" yellow print square

2, 3 - blue prints
4, 5 - yellow prints
6, 7 - blue prints
8, 9 - yellow prints
10, 11 - blue prints

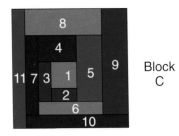

Block B

For each of 20 C Blocks:
- Use the following fabrics in these positions:
  - 1 - 2" blue print square
  - 2 through 11 - assorted blue prints

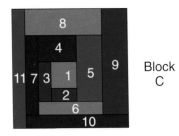

Block C

For 4 Corner Blocks:
- Use the following fabrics in these positions:
  - 1 - 2" yellow print square

2, 3 - blue prints
4, 5 - blue prints
6, 7 - blue prints
8, 9 - yellow prints
10, 11 - blue prints

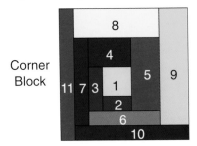

Corner Block

- Baste each foundation in the seam allowance, halfway between the stitching line and the broken line, to hold the fabrics in place, if desired.
- Trim each foundation on the broken line.

ASSEMBLY

- Lay out the 64 blocks in 8 rows of 8, referring to the Assembly Diagram on page 15. Be careful to orient the blocks as shown.
- Stitch the blocks into rows and join the rows.
- Finish the quilt as described in *General Directions*, using the 2 1/2" x 44" blue print strips for the binding.

Assembly Diagram

Full-Size Foundation for Full Circle II: Contrast

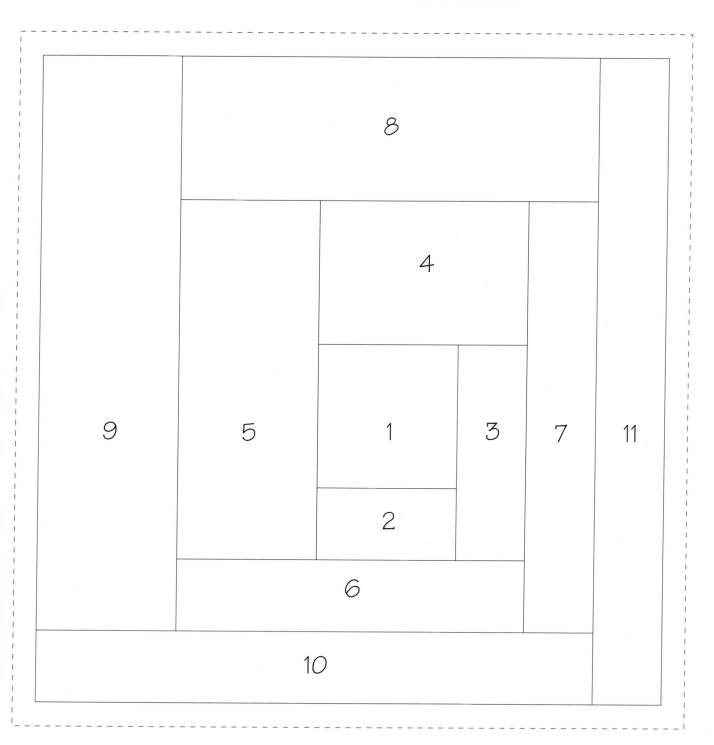

Stars Around the Cabin

Use scraps for a country look!

QUILT SIZE: 55" square
LOG CABIN BLOCK SIZE: 7" square
STAR BLOCK SIZE: 4" square

MATERIALS

Yardage is estimated for 44" fabric.
- Assorted dark prints totaling 1 3/4 yards
- Assorted light prints totaling 2 1/4 yards
- 1 yard blue print for the outer border
NOTE: *This is enough fabric for pieced border strips. If you wish to cut your borders in continuous lengthwise strips, you will need 1 3/4 yards*
- 1/2 yard red print for the binding
- 3 1/4 yards backing fabric
- 59" square of batting

CUTTING

Pattern pieces (on page 20) are full-size and include a 1/4" seam allowance, as do all dimensions given. Stack the pieces and label the stacks as you cut them.

For the Log Cabin blocks:

NOTE: *You may want to cut 14 dark and 11 light 1 1/2" x 44" strips first. Either cut pieces from the strips using templates or rotary cut them to the length given.*

- Cut 16: A, dark prints; or cut 1 1/2" squares
- Cut 16: B, dark prints; or cut 1 1/2" x 2 1/2" strips
- Cut 16: C, dark prints; or cut 1 1/2" x 3 1/2" strips
- Cut 16: D, dark prints; or cut 1 1/2" x 4 1/2" strips
- Cut 16: E, dark prints; or cut 1 1/2" x 5 1/2" strips
- Cut 16: F, dark prints; or cut 1 1/2" x 6 1/2" strips
- Cut 16: G, dark prints; or cut 1 1/2" x 7 1/2" strips
- Cut 16: A, light prints; or cut 1 1/2" squares
- Cut 16: B, light prints; or cut 1 1/2" x 2 1/2" strips
- Cut 16: C, light prints; or cut 1 1/2" x 3 1/2" strips
- Cut 16: D, light prints; or cut 1 1/2" x 4 1/2"

strips
- Cut 16: E, light prints; or cut 1 1/2" x 5 1/2" strips
- Cut 16: F, light prints; or cut 1 1/2" x 6 1/2" strips

For the Stars:

- Cut 28: H, dark prints; or cut 2 1/2" squares
- Cut 224: A, dark prints; or cut 1 1/2" squares
- Cut 112: A, light prints; or cut 1 1/2" squares
- Cut 112: B, light prints; or cut 1 1/2" x 2 1/2" strips

For the Sawtooth Border:

- Cut 41: J, dark prints; or cut 2 7/8" squares
- Cut 41: J, light prints; or cut 2 7/8" squares
- Cut 2: H, light prints; or cut 2 1/2" squares

Also cut:

- Cut 1 1/2"-wide strips, light prints, in various lengths to total 560" in length, for the borders
- Cut 28: 1 3/8" x 4 1/2" strips, light prints
- Cut 6: 4 1/2" x 44" strips, blue print, for the outer border
- Cut 6: 2 1/2" x 44" strips, red print, for the binding

PIECING

For each of 16 Log Cabin blocks:

- Sew a light print A to a dark print A.
- Sew a light print B to the pieced unit.

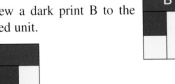

- Sew a dark print B to the pieced unit.

- Sew a dark print C to the pieced unit.

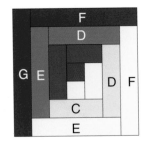

- Sew a light print C to the pieced unit.

- Continue adding light and dark strips in alphabetical order around the block, as shown.

- Lay out the Log Cabin blocks in 4 row of 4, as shown. Sew the blocks into row and join the rows to make the quilt center Set it aside.

- Join enough 1 1/2"-wide light pri strips, end to end, to make a border 34" length. Make 4.
- Measure the quilt. Trim 2 borders that measurement. Sew them to opposi sides of the quilt.
- Measure the quilt including the bo ders. Trim the remaining borders to th measurement. Sew them to the remaini sides of the quilt.

For each of 28 Star blocks:

- Draw a diagonal line, from corner corner, on the wrong side of each remai

*Jennifer Rourke and Jane Walck of Barn Door Designs created **"Stars Around the Cabin"** (57" square). Jennifer used light and dark fabrics from her "stash" and many different prints to create a scrappy look. Two traditional block designs and a Sawtooth border make this a lively quilt!*

...g dark print A.

• Place a dark print A on a light print B, ...ght sides together, and sew on the drawn ...ne, as shown. Trim the ...am allowance to 1/4" and ...ess toward the dark print. ...lake 4.

• Place a dark print A on the B, as shown. Sew on the line. Trim and press, as before, to complete a star-point

unit. Make 4.

• Lay out a dark print H, 4 star-point units and 4 light print A's. Sew them into rows and join the rows to make a Star block.

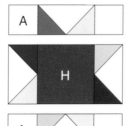

• Lay out 6 Star blocks and seven 1 3/8" x 4 1/2" light print strips, beginning and ending with a light print strip, as shown. Join them to make a border. Make 2.

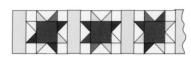

• Sew the borders to opposite sides of the quilt.
• Lay out 8 Star blocks and seven 1 3/8"

(Continued on page 21)

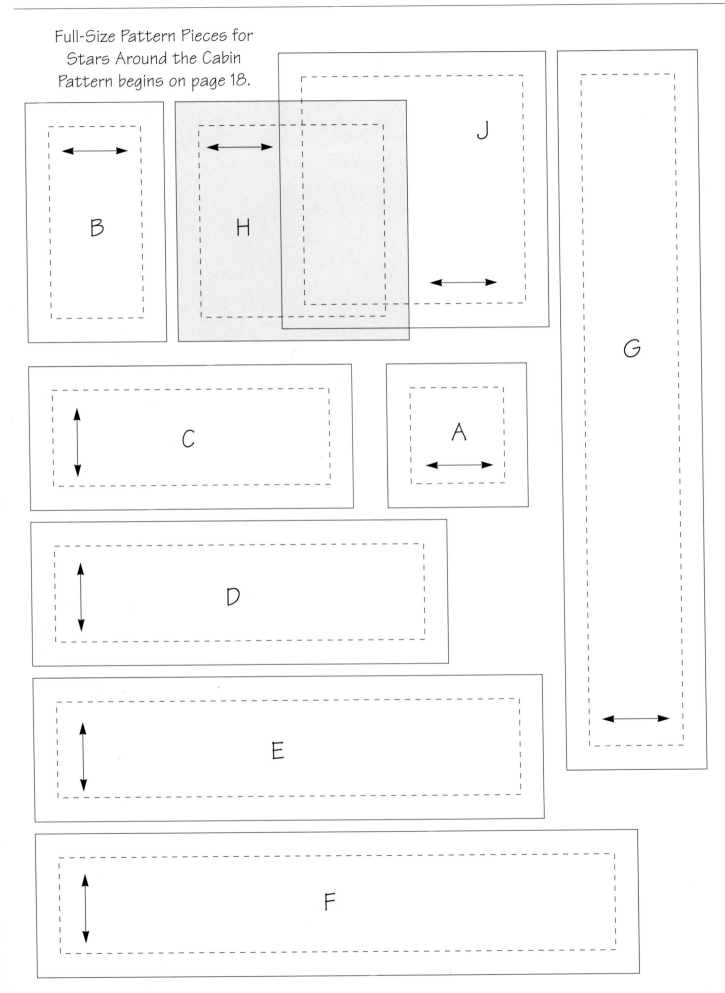

Full-Size Pattern Pieces for
Stars Around the Cabin
Pattern begins on page 18.

B

H

J

G

C

A

D

E

F

x 4 1/2" light print strips, beginning and ending with a Star block. Join them to make a border. Make 2.
• Sew these borders to the remaining sides of the quilt.
• Join enough 1 1/2"-wide light print strips, end to end, to make a pieced border 44" in length. Make 4.
• Measure the quilt. Trim 2 pieced borders to that measurement and sew them to opposite sides of the quilt.
• Measure the quilt including the borders. Trim the 2 remaining pieced borders to that measurement. Sew them to the remaining sides of the quilt.

For the Sawtooth Border:
• Draw a line on the wrong side of each light print J.
• Place a light print J on a dark print J, right sides together. Sew 1/4" away from the drawn line on both sides. Make 41.

• Cut the squares on the drawn lines to yield 82 pieced squares. Press the seam allowances toward the dark print.
• Lay out 20 pieced squares and join them to make a Sawtooth border, as shown. Make 2.

• Sew the Sawtooth borders to opposite sides of the quilt, keeping the dark triangles against the quilt. Refer to the photo as needed.
• Lay out 21 pieced squares and 2 light print H's. Join them to make a Sawtooth border, as shown. Make 2.

• Sew the Sawtooth borders to the remaining sides of the quilt in the same manner.
• Join enough 1 1/2"-wide light print strips, end to end, to make a pieced border 50" in length. Make 4.
• Measure the quilt. Trim 2 pieced borders to that measurement and sew them to opposite sides of the quilt.
• Measure the quilt including the borders. Trim the 2 remaining pieced borders to that measurement. Sew them to the remaining sides of the quilt.
• Cut 2 of the 4 1/2" x 44" blue print strips in half crosswise. Sew one of the resulting strips to each of the remaining 4 1/2" x 44" blue print strips to make 4 borders.
• Measure the quilt. Trim 2 blue borders to that measurement. Sew them to opposite sides of the quilt.
• Measure the width of the quilt, including the borders. Trim the remaining blue borders to that measurement. Sew them to the remaining sides of the quilt.
• Finish the quilt as described in *General Directions,* using the 2 2" x 44" blue strips for the binding.

Setting Variations for Log Cabin Quilts

Try different settings for your log cabin blocks.

Log Cabin blocks can be arranged in many ways to create secondary designs. Here are six traditional settings for you to use as a starting point. Try your own new ideas on a flannel wall or floor before sewing the blocks together.

Barn Raising

Straight Furrows

Streak of Lightening

Light and Dark Variation

Sunshine and Shadows

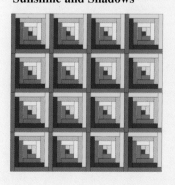

Arrows

Crazy Maze Log Cabin

Feel the warmth of sunlight dancing among fallen leaves in this beauty!

QUILT SIZE: 53" square
BLOCK SIZE: 6" square

MATERIALS

Yardage is estimated for 44" fabric.
- 8 fat quarters (18" x 22") of assorted bright prints including yellow, green, dark red and blue
- 3/4 yard medium autumn leaf print
- 2 1/4 yards dark autumn leaf print
- 3 1/4 yards backing fabric
- 57" square of batting

CUTTING

Dimensions include a 1/4" seam allowance.
- Cut 64: 1 3/4" x 22" strips, assorted bright prints
- Cut 9: 1 3/4" x 44" strips, medium leaf print
- Cut 24: 1 3/4" x 44" strips, dark leaf print
- Cut 12: 2 1/2" x 44" strips, dark leaf print, for the border and binding

PIECING

For 36 A Blocks:

NOTE: *You will use a 1 3/4" x 22" bright print strip and approximately half of a 1 3/4" x 44" medium or dark leaf print strip for each block.*
- Cut a 1 3/4" square from a bright print strip and a leaf print strip. Place them right sides together and sew them to make a pieced unit. Press the seam allowance toward the leaf print.
- Placing the bright print square at the top, sew the unit to the leaf print strip, right sides together along the pieced unit's length.
- Cut the leaf print strip even with the pieced unit, as shown. Press the seam allowance toward the leaf print to complete round 1.

- Positioning the unit so that the last fabric added is away from you, sew the pieced unit to the bright print strip, right sides together. Cut the bright print strip even with the unit and press the seam allowance toward the bright print.

- Positioning the unit so that the last fabric added is toward you, sew the pieced unit to the bright print strip. Cut and press as before to complete round 2 as shown.

- Positioning the unit so that the last fabric added is away from you, sew the pieced unit to the leaf print strip, right sides together. Cut the leaf print strip even with the unit and press the seam allowance toward the leaf print.
- Positioning the unit so that the last fabric added is toward you, sew the pieced unit to the leaf print strip. Cut and press as before to complete round 3.
- Positioning the unit so that the last fabric added is away from you, sew the pieced unit to the bright print strip. Cut the bright print strip even with the unit and press the seam allowance toward the bright print.
- Positioning the unit so that the last fabric added is toward you, sew the pieced unit to the bright print strip. Cut and press as before to complete round 4.

- Make 28 A blocks with the dark leaf print and 8 with the medium leaf print.

Block A

For 28 B Blocks:
- Cut a 1 3/4" square from a leaf print strip and a bright print strip. Sew them together and press the seam allowance toward the bright print.

- Placing the leaf print square at the top, sew the unit to the bright print strip right sides together along the pieced unit's length.
- Cut the bright print strip even with the pieced unit, as shown. Press the seam allowance toward the bright print to complete round 1.
- Positioning the unit so that the last fabric added is away from you, sew the pieced unit to the leaf print strip. Cut the leaf print strip even with the unit and press the seam allowance toward the leaf print.
- Positioning the unit so that the last fabric added is toward you, sew the pieced unit to the leaf print strip. Cut and press as before to complete round 2.
- Positioning the unit so that the last fabric added is away from you, sew the pieced unit to the bright print strip. Cut the bright print strip even with the unit and press the seam allowance toward the bright print.
- Positioning the unit so that the last fabric added is toward you, sew the pieced unit to the bright print strip. Cut and press as before to complete round 3.
- Positioning the unit so that the last fabric added is away from you, sew the pieced unit to the leaf print strip. Cut the leaf print strip even with the unit and press the seam allowance toward the leaf print.
- Positioning the unit so that the last fabric added is toward you, sew the pieced unit to the leaf print strip. Cut and press as before to complete round 4.

- Make 19 B blocks with the dark leaf print and 9 with the medium leaf print.

Block B

By using simple Half-log Cabin blocks, bright colors and autumn leaf prints, you can almost get lost in the warmth and exuberance of "Crazy Maze Log Cabin" (53" square.) The spontaneity of the color placement creates excitement for a bed or the walls of your home.

ASSEMBLY

Lay out the 64 Half-log Cabin blocks in rows of 8, referring to the photo for placement ideas. NOTE: *A piece of flannel stapled to a wall will allow you to play with your design until you are satisfied with the arrangement.*

Sew the blocks into rows and join the rows.

• Sew the six 2 1/2" x 44" dark leaf print strips together, end to end, to make a long pieced strip.
• Measure the quilt. From the long pieced strip, cut two border strips to that measurement and sew them to opposite sides of the quilt.
• Measure the width of the quilt, including the borders. From the remainder of the

long pieced strip, cut two border strips to that measurement and sew them to the remaining sides of the quilt.
• Finish the quilt as described in the *General Directions*, using the remaining 2 1/2" x 44" dark leaf print strips for the binding.

Purple Log Cabin

Have a passion for purple? Show it off with this cheerful quilt.

QUILT SIZE: 83 1/2" x 96"
BLOCK SIZE: 12 1/2" square

MATERIALS

Yardage is estimated for 44" fabric.

• 3/4 yard red print, for the block centers and middle border
• 10 fat quarters (18" x 22") light prints
• 10 fat quarters dark prints, including some purple
• 1/2 yard each of two green prints, for the inner border
• 2 1/2 yards purple print, for the outer border and binding
• 5 1/2 yards backing fabric
• 88" x 100" piece of batting

CUTTING

All dimensions include a 1/4" seam allowance. Assign the pieces a letter, as indicated, for easier identification when sewing the blocks.

• Cut 30: 3" squares, red print (A)
• Cut 30: 3" squares, light prints (B)
• Cut 30: 3" x 5 1/2" strips, light prints (C)
• Cut 30: 3" x 8" strips, light prints (F)
• Cut 30: 3" x 10 1/2" strips, light prints (G)
• Cut 30: 3" x 5 1/2" strips, dark prints (D)
• Cut 30: 3" x 8" strips, dark prints (E)
• Cut 30: 3" x 10 1/2" strips, dark prints (H)
• Cut 30: 3" x 13" strips, dark prints (I)

For the borders:

• Cut 4: 2 1/2" x 44" strips, green print, for the inner border
• Cut 4: 2 1/2" x 44" strips, second green print, for the inner border
• Cut 8: 1 1/2" x 44" strips, red print, for the middle border
• Cut 4: 7 1/2" x 85" strips, purple print, for the outer border
• Cut 5: 2 1/2" x 80" strips, purple print, for the binding

PIECING

• Pick up an A and B, place them right sides together with the B on the top, and stitch them. As you near the end of the seam, pick up another A and B and feed them into the machine, chain sewing them. Chain sew all the A's and B's in this manner.

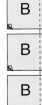

• Clip the threads between the AB units, and press the seam allowances toward B.

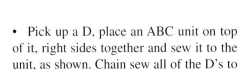

• Pick up a C, place an AB unit on top of it, right sides together and stitch, as shown. Chain sew all of the C's to AB units.

• Clip threads and press the seam allowances toward C.

• Pick up a D, place an ABC unit on top of it, right sides together and sew it to the unit, as shown. Chain sew all of the D's to the pieced units.

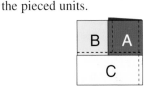

• Clip threads and press the seam allowances toward D.
• Pick up an E, place the ABCD unit on top if it, right sides together and sew it to the unit, as shown. Chain sew all of the E's to the pieced units.

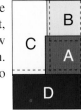

• Clip the threads and press the seam allowance toward E. You have completed one round. The colors are set with lights on two adjacent sides and darks on the opposite sides.
• Complete a second round adding two lights, F and G, and two darks, H and I, as before, to complete a Log Cabin block. Make 30.

ASSEMBLY

• Referring to the photo for light/dark placement, lay out the blocks in 6 rows of 5.
• Stitch the blocks into rows and join the rows.
• Sew a 2 1/2" x 44" green print strip and a 2 1/2" x 44" second green print strip together, end to end, to make a border. Make 4.
• Measure the length of the quilt. Trim green borders to that measurement. Sew them to the long sides of the quilt.
• Measure the width of the quilt, including the borders. Trim the remaining green borders to that measurement. Sew them to the remaining sides of the quilt.
• In the same manner, sew two 1 1/2" x 44" red print strips together, end to end, to make a border. Make 4.
• Measure the length of the quilt, trim red print borders to that measurement and sew them to the long sides of the quilt.
• Measure the width of the quilt, including the borders, trim the remaining red print borders to that measurement and sew them to the remaining sides of the quilt.
• Trim two 7 1/2" x 85" purple print strips to fit the quilt's length and sew them to the long sides of the quilt.
• Trim the remaining 7 1/2" x 85" purple print strips to fit the quilt's width and sew them to the remaining sides of the quilt.
• Finish the quilt as described in *General Directions*, using the 2 1/2" x 80" purple print strips for the binding.

*purple's not your passion, substitute your favorite color in this charming country-style "**Purple Log Cabin**" (83 1/2" x 96") quilt. It's perfect ...or a first project, as there are only two rounds in each block.*

Victorian Christmas Log Cabin

Timeless Log Cabin blocks and your prettiest Christmas prints—an unbeatable combination!

QUILT SIZE: 65 1/2" square
BLOCK SIZE: 10 1/2" square

MATERIALS

Yardage is estimated for 44" fabric. You may choose to substitute other colors.

• Christmas print fabric with 6 pictorial motifs that will fit a 2 1/2" square, 12 motifs that will fit a 4 1/2" square and 7 motifs that will fit a 6 1/2" square; yardage will depend on the number of usable motifs on the fabric.
• 1/4 yard each of 8 different deep reds
• 1/4 yard each of 8 different deep greens
• 3/8 yard pink solid for the cornerstones
• 1/2 yard light-colored print for the piping frames
• 3/8 yard light gray print for the inner border
• 3/8 yard dark red print for the middle border
• 1 3/4 yards dark green print for the outer border and binding
• 4 yards backing fabric
• 70" square of batting
• Clear plastic template material

PREPARATION

• Cut clear plastic templates in the following sizes– 3" square, 5" square and 7" square.
• Use the templates to "audition" motifs for your quilt. Center a template over a motif. The motif must fit inside the square, with at least a 1/4" margin on all sides for the seam allowance.

CUTTING

Dimensions include a 1/4" seam allowance.
• Cut 4: 1 1/2" x 44" strips from each of the 8 deep red fabrics
• Cut 4: 1 1/2" x 44" strips from each of the 8 deep green fabrics
• Cut 8: 1 1/2" x 44" strips, pink, from them cut one hundred eighty 1 1/2" squares for the block cornerstones
• Cut 13: 1" x 44" strips, light-colored

print for the piping frame
• Cut 6: 3" pictorial motif squares
• Cut 12: 5" pictorial motif squares
• Cut 7: 7" pictorial motif squares
• Cut 16: 1 1/2" x 10" strips, light gray print
• Cut 4: 1 1/2 " x 11" strips, light gray print
• Cut 16: 1 1/2" x 10" strips, dark red print
• Cut 4: 1 1/2" x 11" strips, dark red print
• Cut 2: 1 1/2" x 2 1/2" rectangles, dark red print
• Cut 2: 1 1/2" squares, dark red print
• Cut 8: 4 1/2" x 44" strips, dark green print for the outer border
• Cut 7: 3" x 44" strips, dark green print for the binding

PIPING FRAMES

• Fold the 1" x 44" strips of light-colored print in half lengthwise, right side out and press.
HINT: *Spray starch the strips and pictorial squares to make it easier to stitch them.*
• Place a folded strip on one side of a pictorial motif square, matching raw edges. Pin the strip in place.
• Baste the folded strip to the square using a 1/8" seam allowance. Trim the end of the strip even with the side of the square. In the same manner, sew a second folded strip to the opposite side of the square.

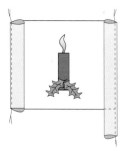

• Sew strips to the remaining sides of the pictorial square, as before. Make 25.

PIECING

NOTE: *Study the block diagrams shown on page 28 before piecing, and refer to them as needed. Centers are indicated by the size of template used to cut them. The 2 1/2" center and 6 1/2" center blocks*

have red fabrics on the lower left side. The 4 1/2" center blocks have green on the lower left side.

For a block with a 2 1/2" finished center
• Lay a 1 1/2" x 44" red print strip on top of a framed 3" pictorial square, right side together. Position the strip along the left side of the picture.
• Sew through all thicknesses. Trim the red print strip even with the edge of the block. Press the strip away from the center.

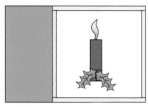

• Using the same color strip, add a second "log." With right sides together, place the strip along the bottom edge of the pictorial square. Sew and trim, as before. Press the strip away from the center.

• Sew a 1 1/2" pink cornerstone square to each end of a 1 1/2" x 44" green print strip. Press the seams toward the green strip.

• Place one end of the green print strip, with a cornerstone along the right edge of the pictorial square, right sides together. Stitch, trim and press, as shown.

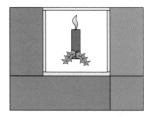

"Victorian Christmas Log Cabin" (65 1/2" square) was made by Harriet Schoeninger of Nashotah, Wisconsin. Harriet used Log Cabin blocks to showcase printed motifs cut from Jinny Beyer's nostalgic Yuletide fabric. Harriet credits a quilt made by her long-time friend Vicki Moskiewicz as the inspiration for this design with its block centers of various sizes.

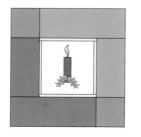

• In the same manner, place the opposite end of the green print strip with a cornerstone along the top edge of the pictorial frame. Stitch, trim and press, as before.

You have completed the first round.
• Continue adding "logs" in the same manner. Blocks with the 2 1/2" finished center have 4 rounds of logs added. Those with a 4 1/2" finished center have 3 rounds, and those with a 6 1/2" fin-

ished center, have 2 rounds. See the block diagrams below. Complete all 25 blocks.

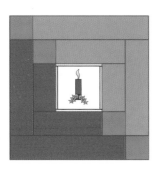

ASSEMBLY

• Referring to the photo, lay out the blocks in 5 rows of 5, making sure that the pictorial motifs are right side up. Stitch the blocks into rows, and join the rows.

For the inner border:

• Lay out four 1 1/2" x 10" light gray strips and four 1 1/2" square pink cornerstones alternately in a row. Add a 1 1/2" x 11" light gray strip to the end with the cornerstone to make a pieced inner border. Make 4.
• Mark the 11" strip in each pieced inner border with a safety pin or a colored thread.
• Stitch a pieced inner border to the right side of the quilt, with the 11" strip toward the top.

• Stitch a second pieced inner border to the left side of the quilt, with the 11" strip toward the bottom.
• Sew a 1 1/2" pink cornerstone square to both ends of a remaining pieced inner border to make a long inner border. Make 2.
• Stitch a long pieced border to the top edge of the quilt, with the 11" strip toward the right.
• Stitch the remaining long pieced border to the bottom of the quilt, with the 11" strip toward the left.

For the middle border:

• Lay out four 1 1/2" x 10" dark red print strips and four 1 1/2" pink cornerstone squares alternately in a row. Add a 1 1/2" x 11" dark red print strip to the end with the cornerstone to make a pieced middle border. Mark the 11" strip as before. Make 4. Set 2 aside.
• Sew a 1 1/2" pink cornerstone square to the 11" end of a pieced middle border. Sew a 1 1/2" dark red print square to the pink cornerstone at the 11" end of the pieced middle border to make a long middle border. Make 2.
• Stitch a long middle border to the right side of the quilt, with the dark red square toward the top. Sew the second long middle border to the left side of the quilt with the dark red square toward the bottom.

• Lay out the 2 reserved pieced middle borders.
• Sew a 1 1/2" pink cornerstone square to both ends of a pieced middle border.
• Sew a 1 1/2" x 2 1/2" dark red print strip to the cornerstone at the 11" end to make a middle border. Make 2.
• Stitch a middle border to the top of the quilt, with the 2 1/2" dark red print strip to the right.
• Stitch the remaining middle border to the bottom of the quilt with the 2 1/2" dark red print strip to the left.

For the outer border:

• Join two 4 1/2" x 44" dark green print strips together, end to end, to make a outer border. Make 4.
• Measure the length of the quilt. Trim pieced outer borders to that measurement. Sew them to the sides of the quilt.
• Measure the width of the quilt including the borders. Trim the 2 remaining pieced outer borders to that measurement. Sew them to the top and bottom of the quilt.
• Finish the quilt as described in *General Directions*, using the 2 1/2" x 44" dark green print strips for the binding.

Green

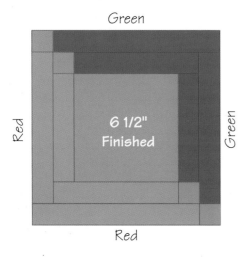

Red | 6 1/2" Finished | Green

Red

Victorian Christmas
Log Cabin Block
Diagrams.

Red

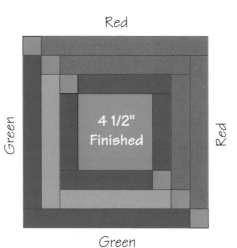

Green | 4 1/2" Finished | Red

Green

Green

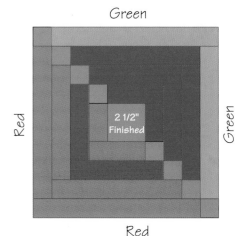

Red | 2 1/2" Finished | Green

Red

Pineapple

Make this distinctive interpretation of an all-time favorite quilt!

*Recreate the sparkle in Beverly Packard's eye-catching **"Pineapple Quilt"** (77" square) using her color formula on page 30.*

Pineapple

QUILT SIZE: 77" square
BLOCK SIZE: 9 1/2" square

MATERIALS

Yardage is estimated for 44" fabric.
NOTE: *See "Color Formula" below for fabric selection.*

• Scraps of red prints, totaling at least 4 1/2 yards
• Scraps of assorted light prints, totaling at least 4 yards
• Scraps of assorted bright color prints, totaling at least 3 1/2 yards
• 1/4 yard first red print
• 1/4 yard second red print
• 1 yard third red print for the binding
• 4 1/2 yards backing fabric
• 81" square of batting
• Paper, muslin or lightweight non-fusible interfacing for foundations
NOTE: *If you use muslin, you'll need 4 1/2 yards. If you use paper, you'll need at least 64 sheets–11" x 17" is a good size.*

CUTTING

Dimensions include a 1/4" seam allowance. Fabric for foundation piecing will be cut as you sew the blocks. Each piece must be at least 1/4" larger on all sides than the section it will cover. Refer to General Directions *as needed.*

• Cut 64: 2" squares, first red print, for position 1.
• Cut 2 1/2"-wide bias strips from the third red print, to total at least 400" in length when sewn end to end, for the binding.

DIRECTIONS

• Follow the foundation piecing instructions in *General Directions* to piece the blocks.

• Trace the pattern 64 times on the foundation material, flipping the pattern where indicated to make a full-size foundation. Transfer all lines and leave a 1" space between foundations. Cut each one out 1/2" beyond the broken line. Number the foundations as indicated on the Block Diagram.

For each of 36 Center blocks:

• Center a 2" red print square right side up over position 1 on the unmarked side of the foundation. Hold this first piece in place with a small dab of glue or a pin.
• Use the following fabrics in these positions:

2 through 5 - bright colors
6 through 9 - lights
10 through 13 - bright colors
14 through 17 - lights
18 through 21 - bright colors
22 through 25 - lights
26 through 29 - bright colors
30 through 33 - lights
34 through 37 - bright colors
38 through 41 - lights

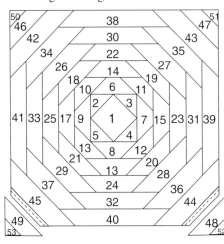

42 through 49 - bright colors
50 through 53 - 1 3/4" squares, second red print

For the Border blocks:

• Mark a dashed line 1/4" outside of the line between positions 45 and 49. Do the same with the line between positions 44 and 48. Trim the 2 corners just outside of the dashed lines, as shown. Make 28. Set aside.
• Mark an X in positions 6, 14, 22, 30 and 38.
• Piece 24 border blocks using red print scraps for all positions except those marked with an X. Use light print scraps in the X positions.

For each of 4 Corner blocks:

• Take the 4 foundations you set aside. Mark a dashed line 1/4" outside of the line between positions 43 and 47. Trim off that corner, as before.
• Use red print scraps for all positions.

ASSEMBLY

• Referring to the photo on page 29, arrange the center blocks in 6 rows of 6. Lay out 6 Border blocks along each side with the light prints turned toward the center. Place a Corner block in each corner.
• Stitch the blocks into rows, then join the rows.
• If you used paper foundations, remove them now.
• Finish the quilt as described in *General Directions,* using the 2 1/2"-wide third red print bias strips for the binding. When you sew the binding to the front of the quilt, the quiltmaker advises making 1/8" tucks on the outside corners and pivoting on the inside corners.

COLOR FORMULA:

The quiltmaker used all print fabrics in these proportions:

For the darker sections:
25% reds from Chinese red to burgundy
25% blues from peacock blue to deep blue-violet
25% greens from yellow green to deep hunter green
5% golds from butterscotch to pumpkin (no yellows)

5% blacks from dark gray to black
5% blue-greens from deep teal to deep turquoise
5% purples from grape to deep violet
5% browns from medium warm brown to darkest browns

For the lighter sections:
Any light gray, beige, taupe, or pastel color printed with any color as long as it reads as a light fabric.

NOTE: *The quiltmaker suggests that white fabrics not be used as the contrast with other fabrics used here is too great and can make the quilt appear "splotchy".*

Half of Full-Size
Foundation for
Pineapple Quilt.

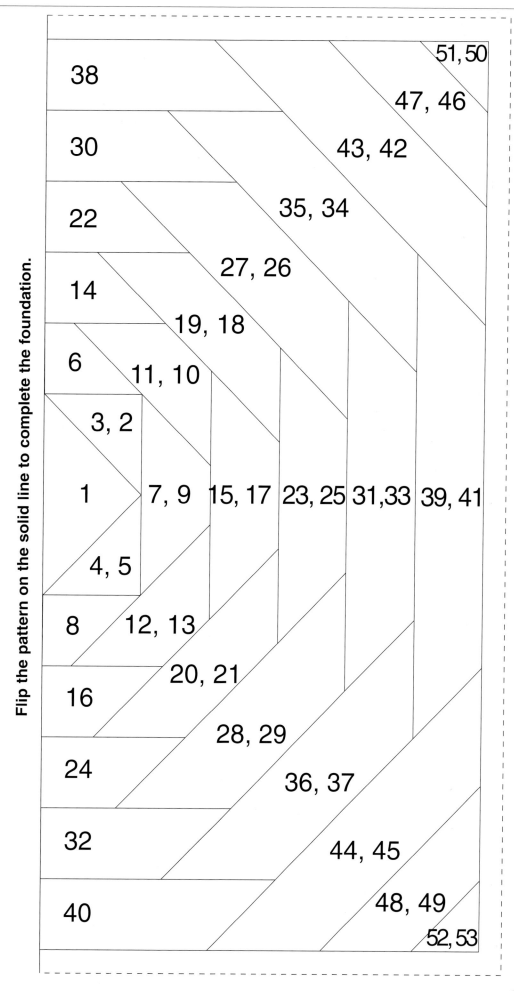

Flip the pattern on the solid line to complete the foundation.

General Directions

FABRIC

Yardage requirements are based on 44" wide fabric. Listed amounts are adequate, but little is allowed for errors. I suggest using 100% cottom fabrics.

CHOOSING A PATTERN

Read through all the directions when choosing a pattern.

PIECING

For machine piecing, set stitch length at 12 stitches per inch and make sure the seamline lies exactly 1/4" from the edge of the fabric. Mark the throat plate with a piece of masking tape placed 1/4" away from the point at which the needle pierces the fabric.

When many of the same pieced unit are required, chain piece them through the machine without stopping. Leave the presser foot down and set pieces against one another. Clip the threads after all the pieces are stitched.

FOUNDATION PIECING

Foundation piecing is a method for making blocks with a high degree of accuracy. For each foundation, trace all of the lines and numbers onto paper, muslin or lightweight non-fusible interfacing. You will need one foundation for each block. The solid line is the stitching line and the broken line is the cutting line. The fabric pieces you select do not have to be cut precisely. Be generous when cutting fabric pieces as excess fabric will be trimmed away after sewing. Your goal is to cut a piece that covers the numbered area and extends into surrounding areas after seams are stitched. Generally, fabric pieces should be large enough to extend 1/2" beyond the seamline on all sides before stitching.

You'll notice that, with certain designs, the foundation pattern is the reverse of the finished block. That's because, when stitching the block, fabric pieces are placed on the unmarked side of the foundation and stitched on the marked side. Center the first piece, right side up, over position 1 on the unmarked side of the foundation. Hold the foundation up to a light to make sure that the raw edges of the fabric extend at least 1/2" beyond the seamline on all sides. Hold this first piece in place with a small dab of glue or a pin if desired. Place the fabric for position 2 on the first piece, right sides together. Turn the foundation over and sew on the line between 1 and 2, extending the stitching past the beginning and end of the line by a few stitches on both ends. Trim the seam allowance to 1/4". Fold the position 2 piece back, right side up, and press. Continue adding pieces to the foundation in the same manner until all positions are covered and the block is complete.

If you are using a muslin or interfacing foundation, it will become a permanent part of the quilt. If you are using paper, it will be removed. However, do not remove the paper until the blocks have been joined together and at least one border has been added, to avoid disturbing the stitches. Use tweezers to carefully remove pieces of the paper. The pieces will be perforated from the stitching and can be gently pulled free.

PRESSING

Press with a dry iron. Press seam allowances toward the darker of the two pieces whenever possible. Otherwise, trim away 1/16" from the darker seam allowance to prevent it from showing through. Press all blocks, sashings and borders before assembling the quilt top.

FINISHING

Marking Quilting Lines

Mark the lines for quilting before basting the quilt together with the batting and backing. I suggest using a very hard (#3 or #4) pencil or a chalk pencil (for darker fabrics) though many marking tools are available. Test any marking method to be sure that the lines will wash out and not damage the fabric in any way. Transfer paper quilting designs by placing fabric over the design and tracing. A light box or a brightly lit window may be necessary when using darker fabrics. Precut plastic stencils allow you to trace the quilting design onto the fabric from the front. check to be sure they fit the area you wish to quilt. Use a ruler to keep lines straight and even when marking grid lines.

Some quilting may be done without marking the top at all. Outline quilting (1/4" from the seamline) or quilting "in the ditch" can be done "by eye". Quilting "in the ditch" is done next to the seam (but not through it) on the patch opposite the pressed seam allowances.

Other straight lines may also be marked as you quilt by using the edge of masking tape as a stitching guide. For simple quilting motifs (hearts, stars, etc.) cut the shapes(s) from clear, sticky-back paper (such as Contact® paper) and position them on your quilt top. These shapes can be reused many times. Do not leave masking tape or adhesive paper on your quilt top overnight. Remove it when you are finished quilting for the day to avoid leaving a residue.

Basting

Cut the batting and backing at least 2" larger than the quilt top on all sides. Place the backing, wrong side up, on a flat surface and anchor in place with masking tape, if possible. Smooth the batting over the backing. Smooth the quilt top, right side up, over the batting. Baste the three layers together with thread or safety pins to form a quilt "sandwich". Beginning at the center of the quilt, baste horizontally first an then vertically. Add additional horizontal and vertical lines of stiches or pins approximately every 6" until the entire top is held together securely. Quilt as desired.

Binding

After the basting is removed, trim excess batting and backing to within 1/4" of the quilt top.

For most straight-edged quilts, a double-fold French binding is an attractive, durable and easy finish. To make 1/2" finished binding, cut each strip 2 1/2" wide. Sew binding strips together with diagonal seams, trim and press seams open.

Fold the binding strip in half lengthwise wrong sides together, and press. Position the binding strip on the right side of the quilt top, aligning the raw edges of the binding with the edge of the quilt top. (not so that all raw edges are even.) Leave approximtaely 6" of binding strip free. Beginning several inches from one corner, stitch the binding to the quilt with a 1/2" seam allowance measuring from the raw edge of the backing. When you reach a corner, stop the stitching line exactly 1/2" from the edge. Backstitch, clip threads and remove the quilt from the machine. Fold the binding up and away, creating a 45° angle, as shown.

Keeping the angled folds secure, fold the binding back down. This fold should be even with the edge of the quilt top. Begin stitching at the fold.

Continue sewing the binding in this manner, stopping 6" from the starting point. To finish, fold both strips back along the edge of the quilt so that the folded edges meet about 3" from both lines of stitching and the binding lies flat on the quilt. Finger press to crease the folds. Cut both strips 1 1/4" from the folds.

Open both strips and place the ends at right angles to each other, right sides together. Fold the bulk of the quilt out of your way. Join the strips with a diagonal seam, as shown.

Trim the seam to 1/4" and press it open. Fold the joined strips so that wrong sides together again. Place the binding flat against the quilt and finish stitching it to the quilt. Trim the layers as needed so that the binding edge will be filled with batting when you fold the binding to the back of the quilt. Blindstitch the binding to the back of the quilt, covering the seamline.

FINISHING THE QUILT

Remove visible markings on the quilt top. Sign and date your quilt.